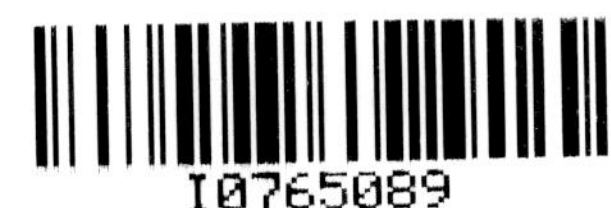

This Christmas coloring book belongs to:

____

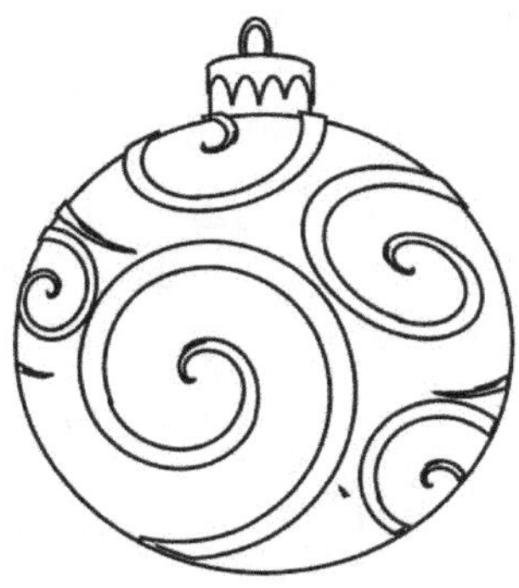

Christmas coloring book for kids ages 2-4

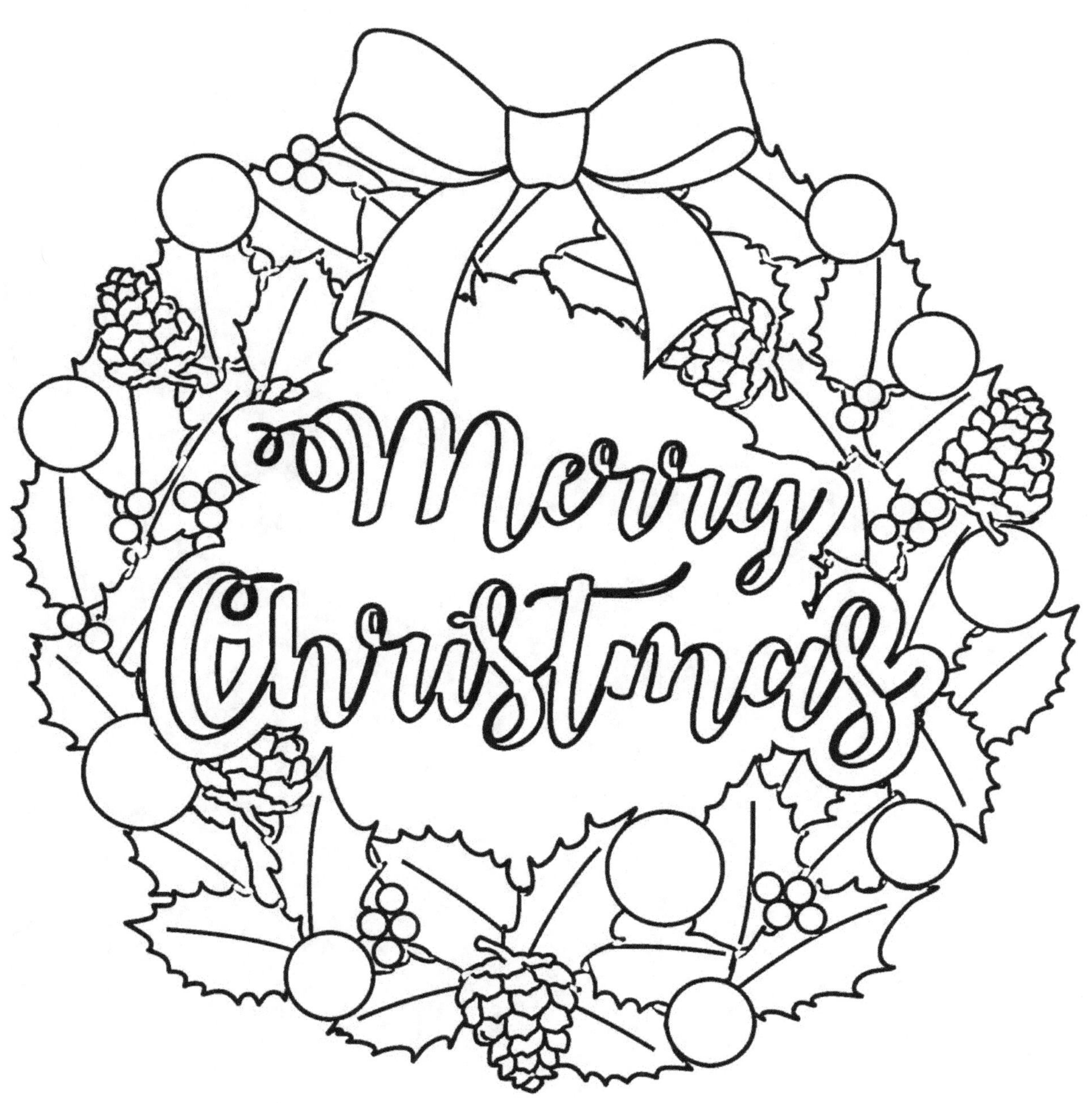

Merry
Christmas

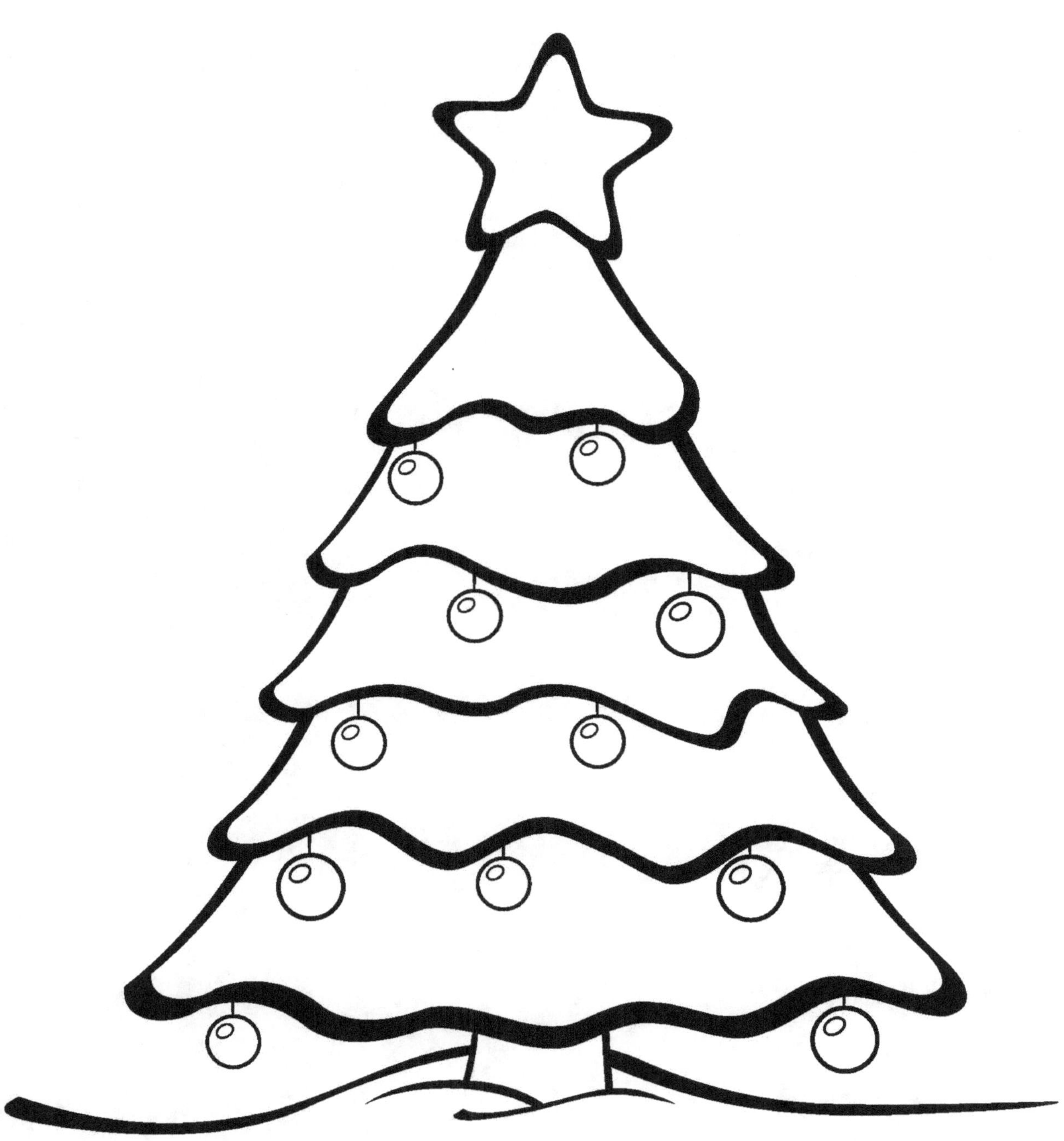

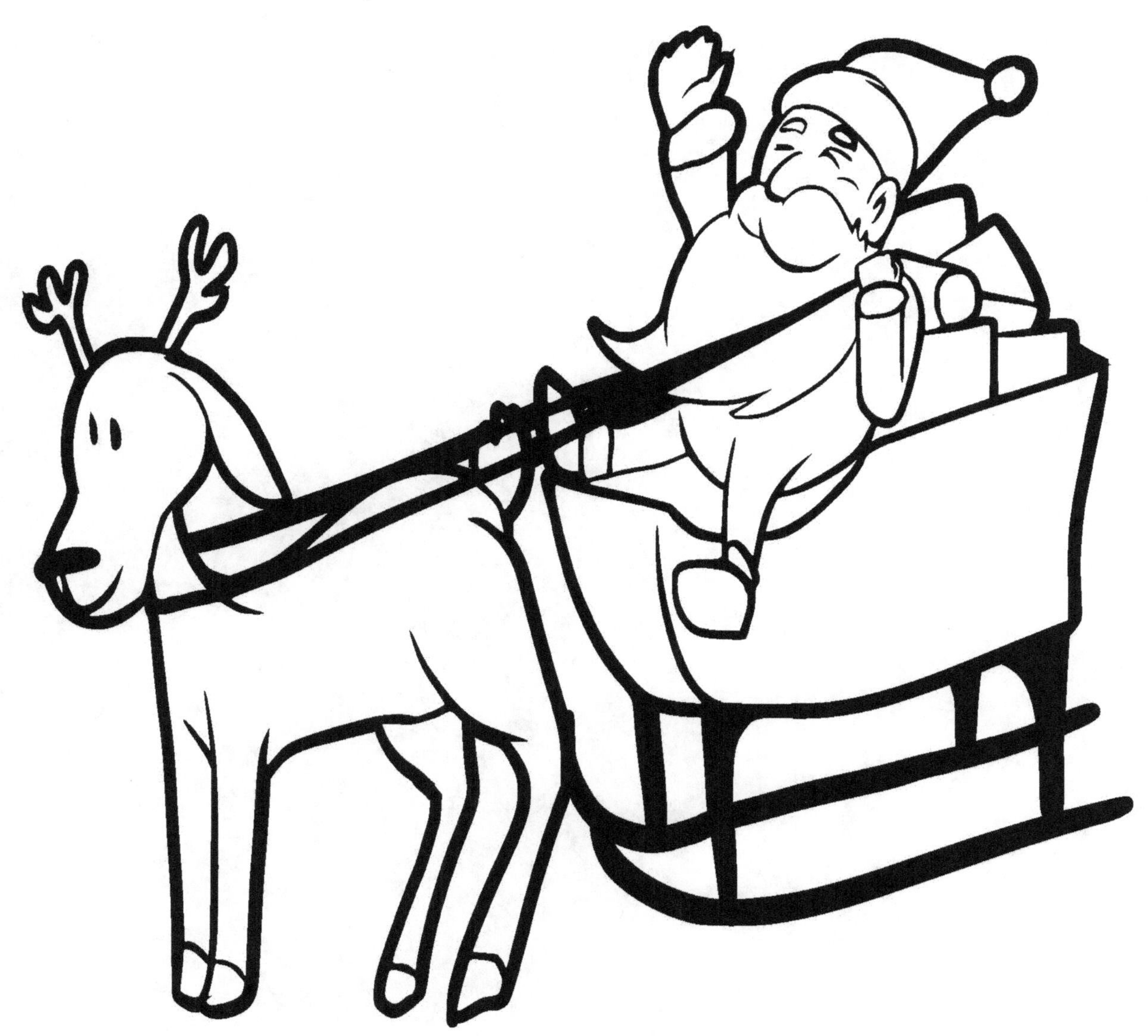

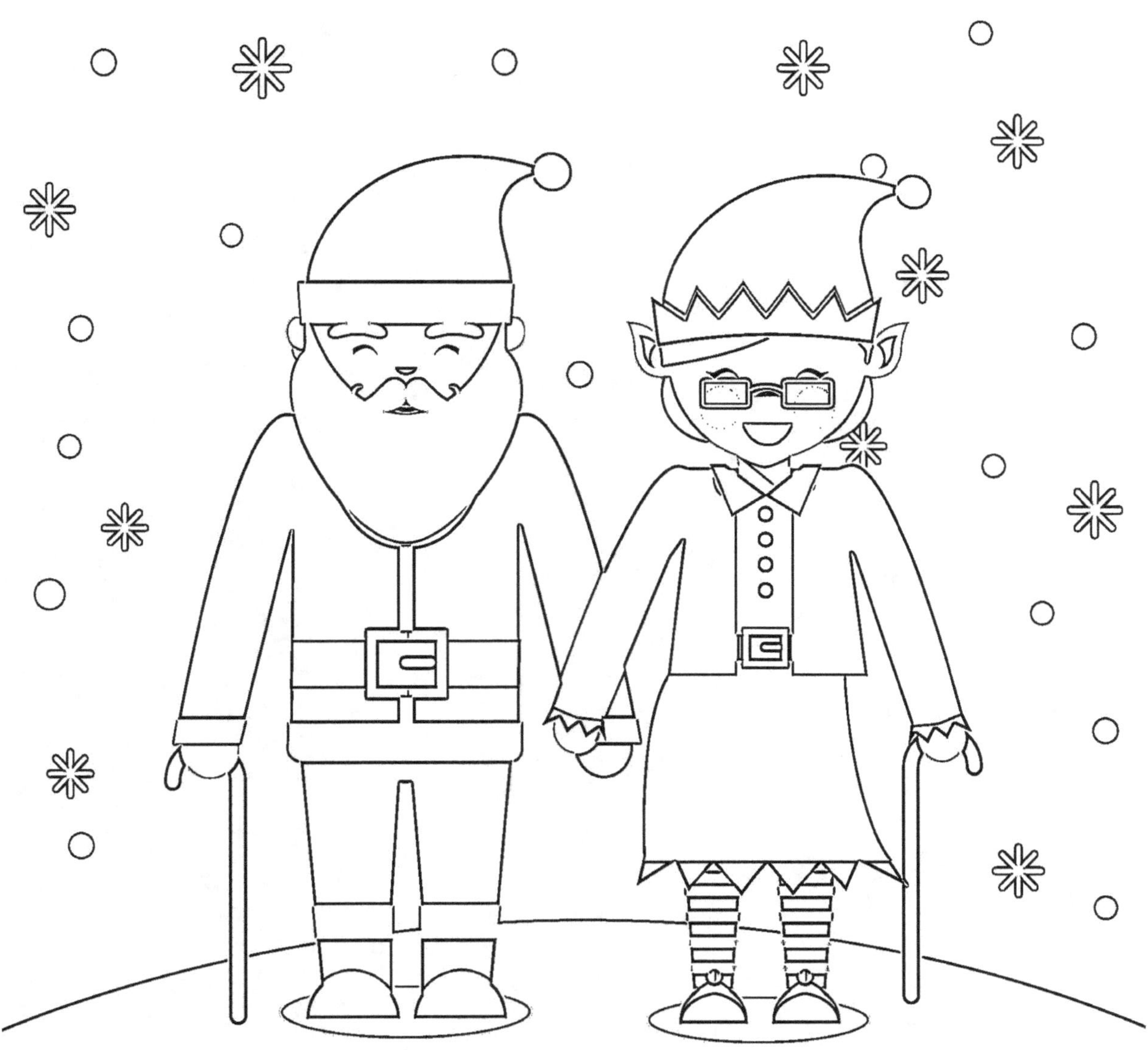

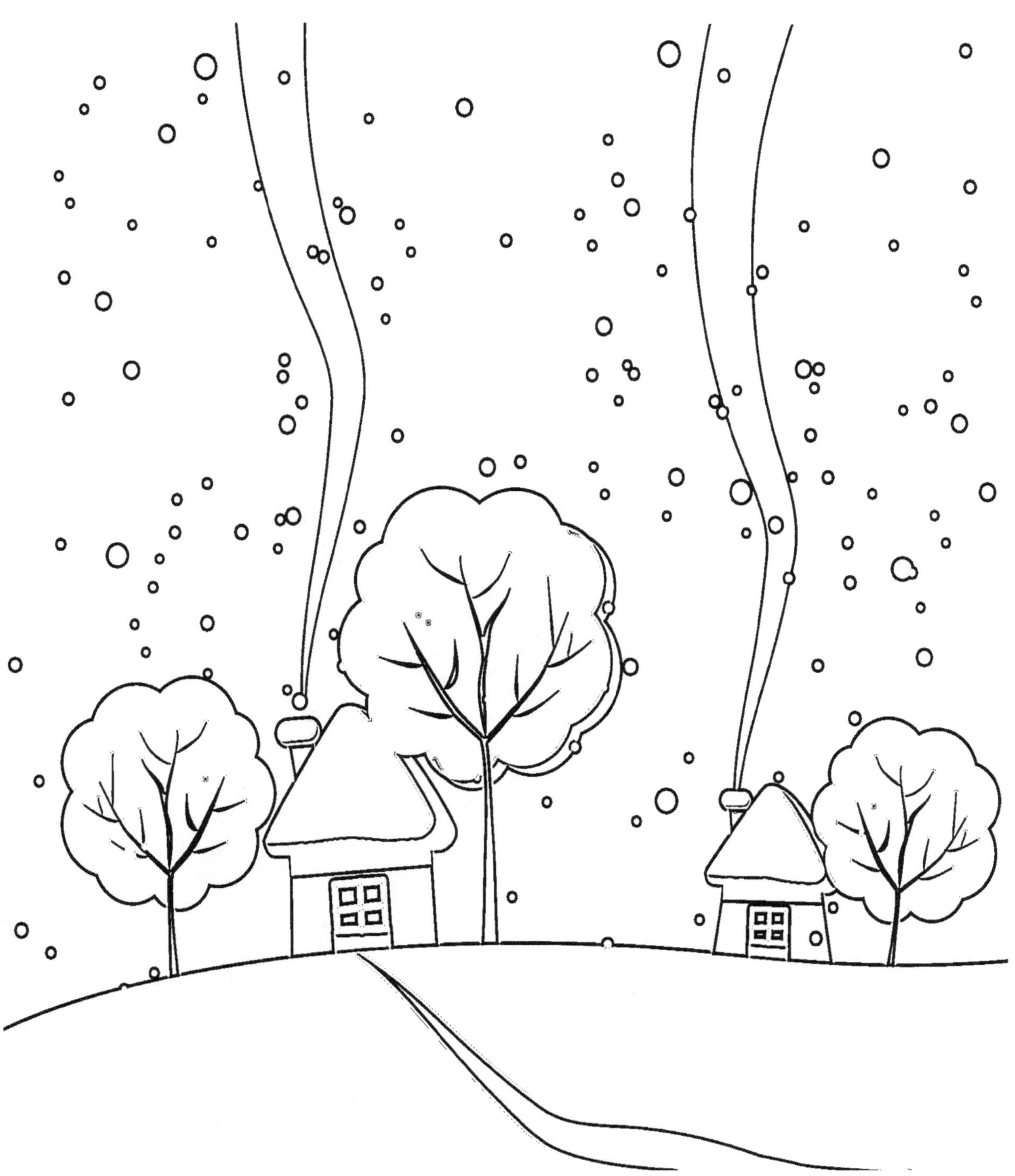

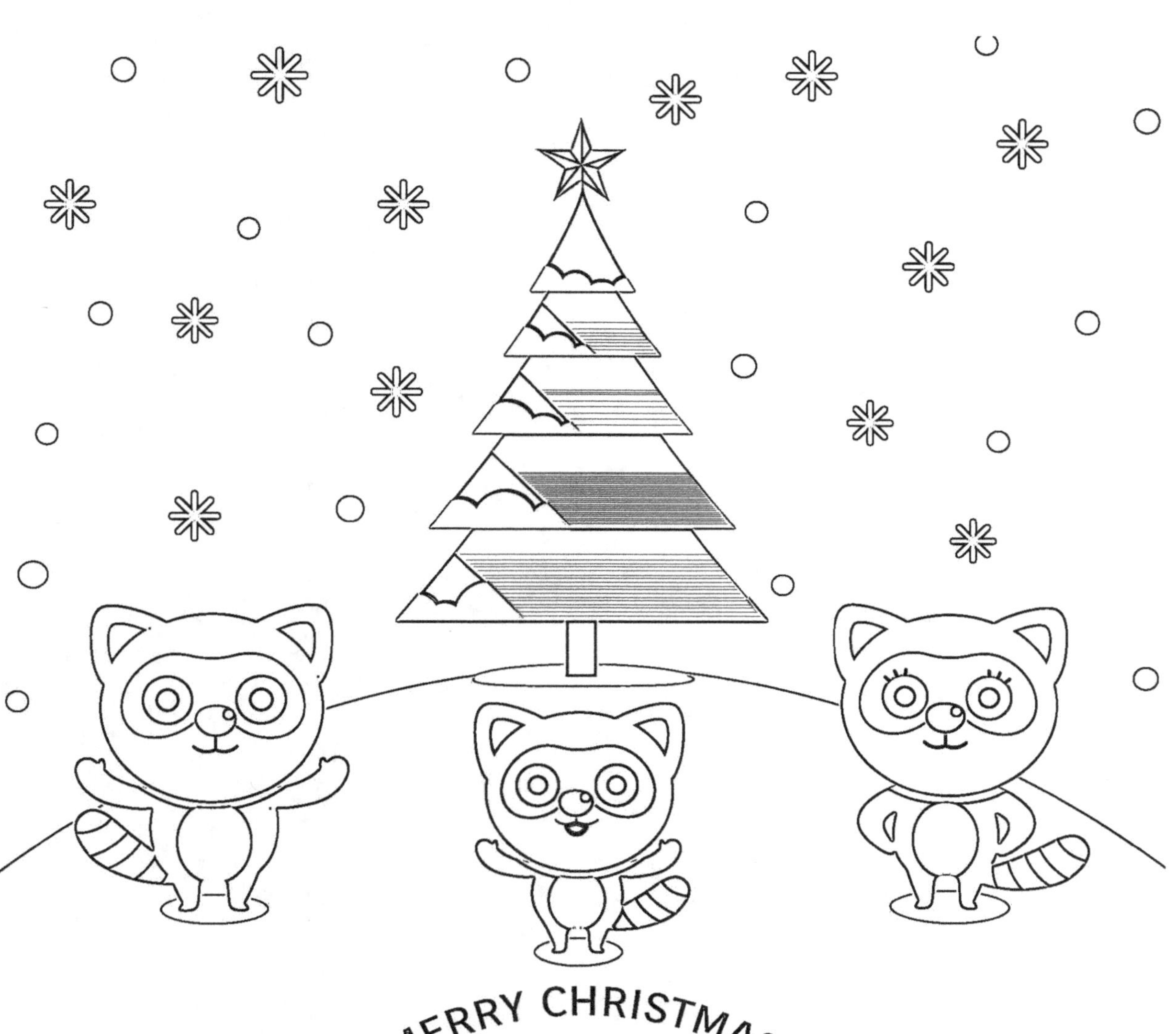

MERRY CHRISTMAS
★ HAPPY NEW YEAR ★

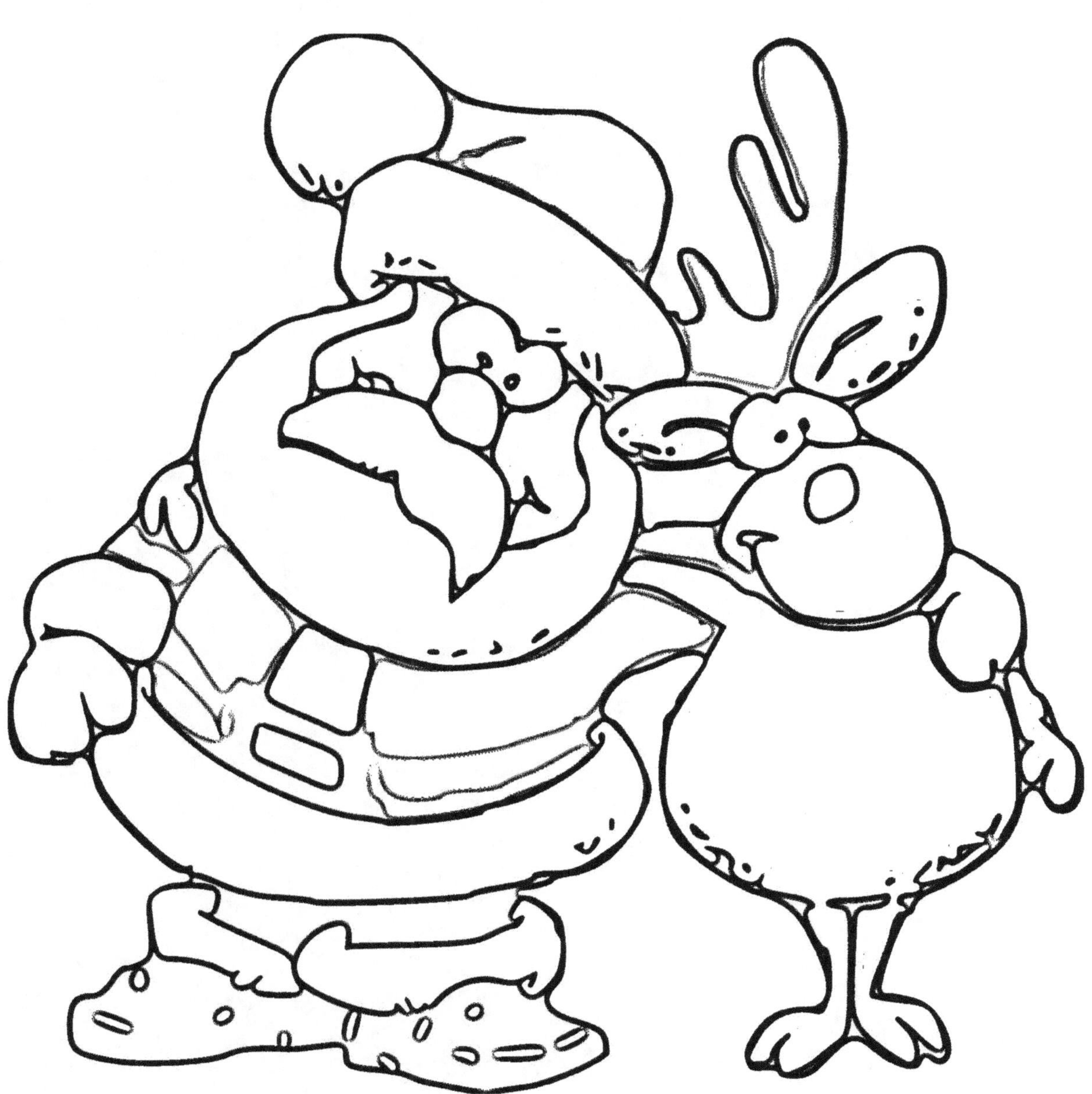

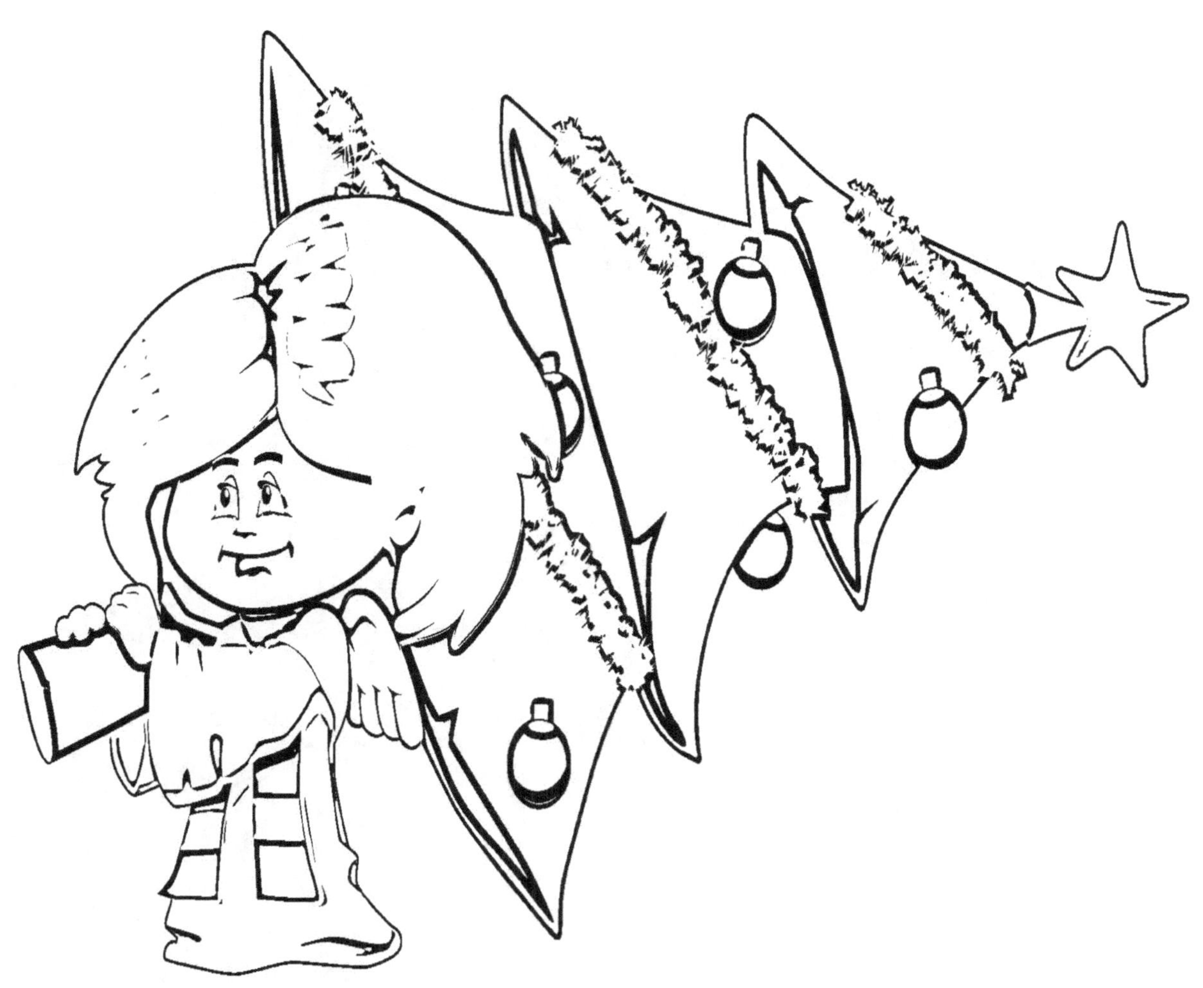

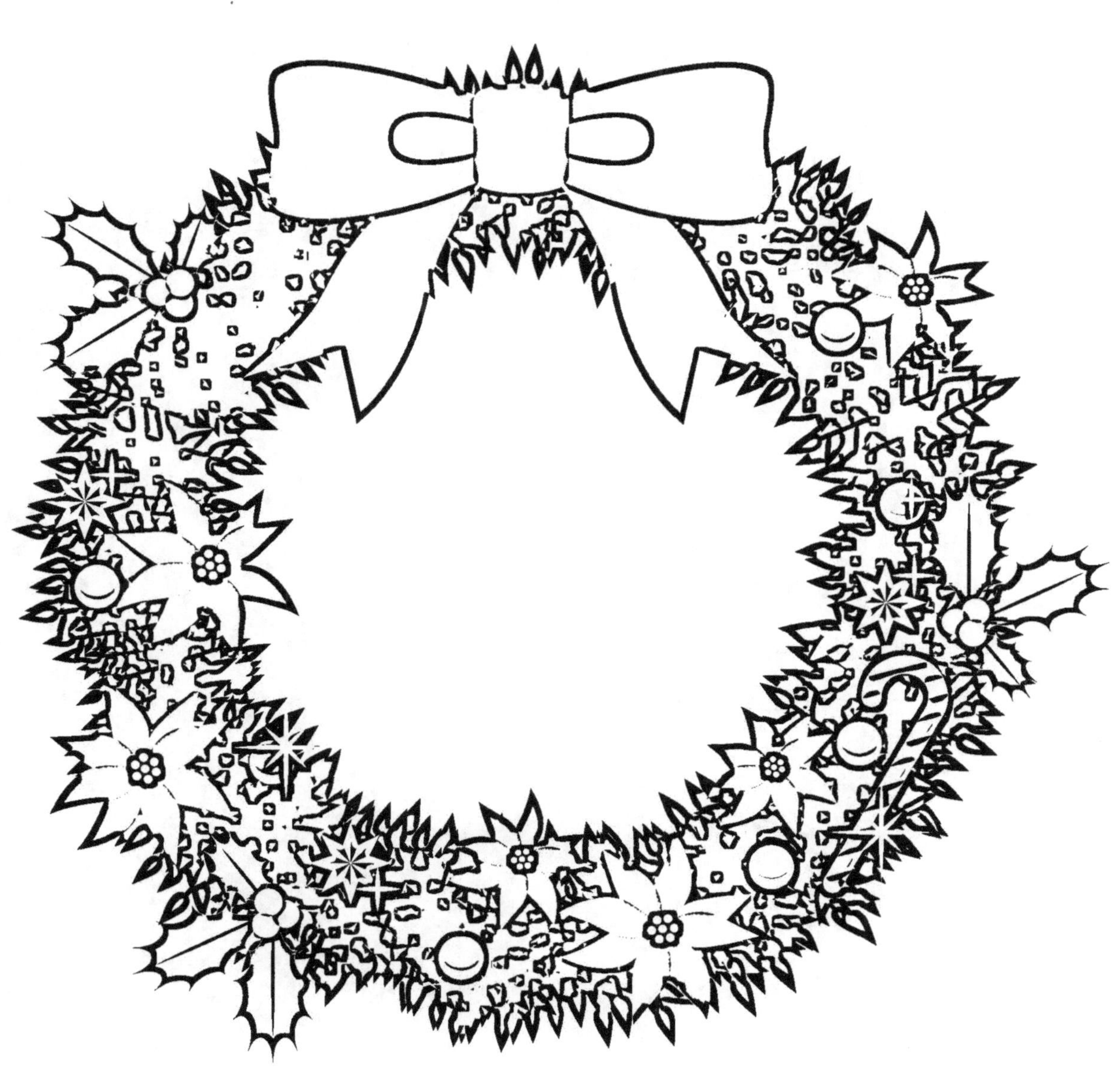

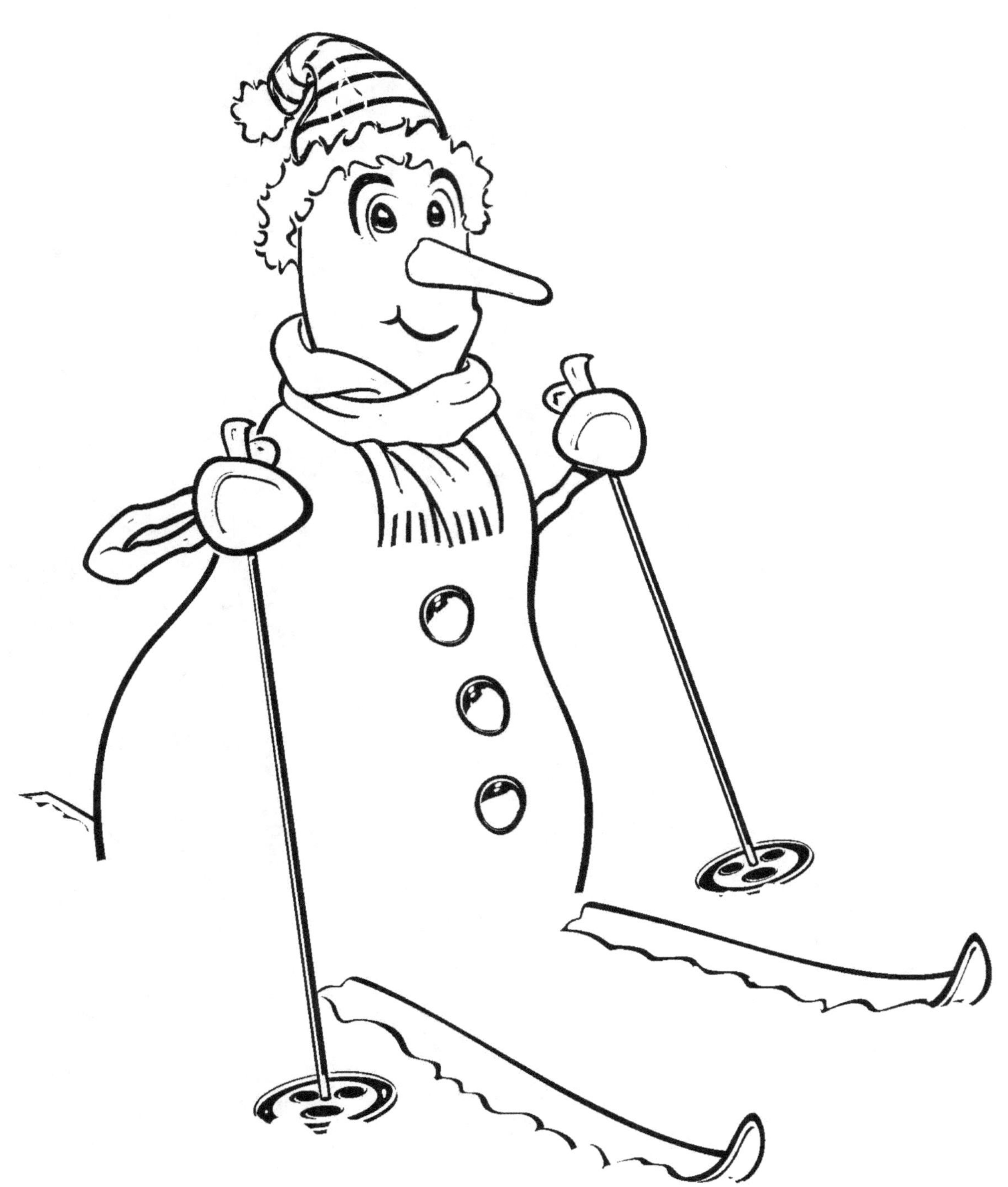

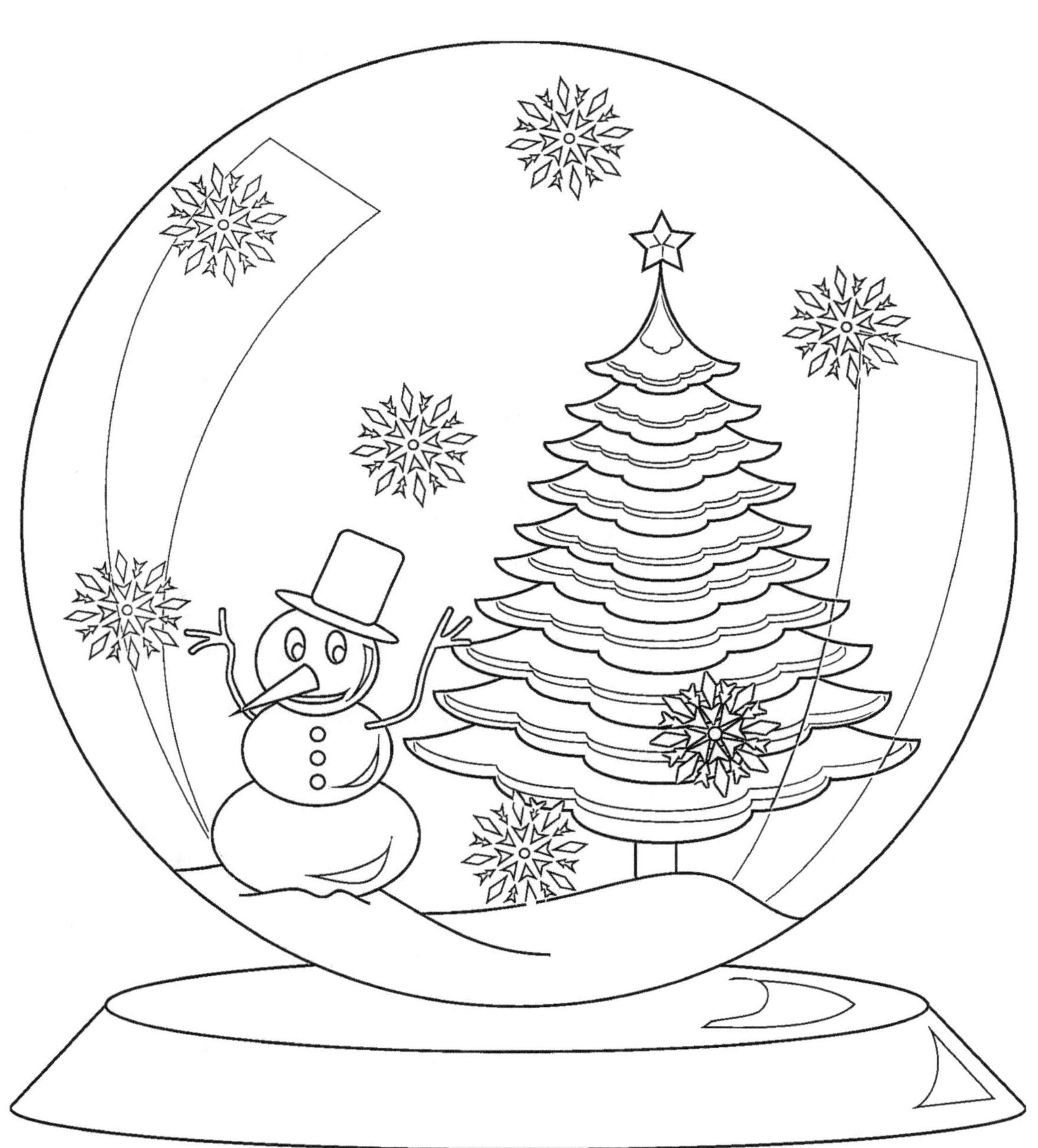

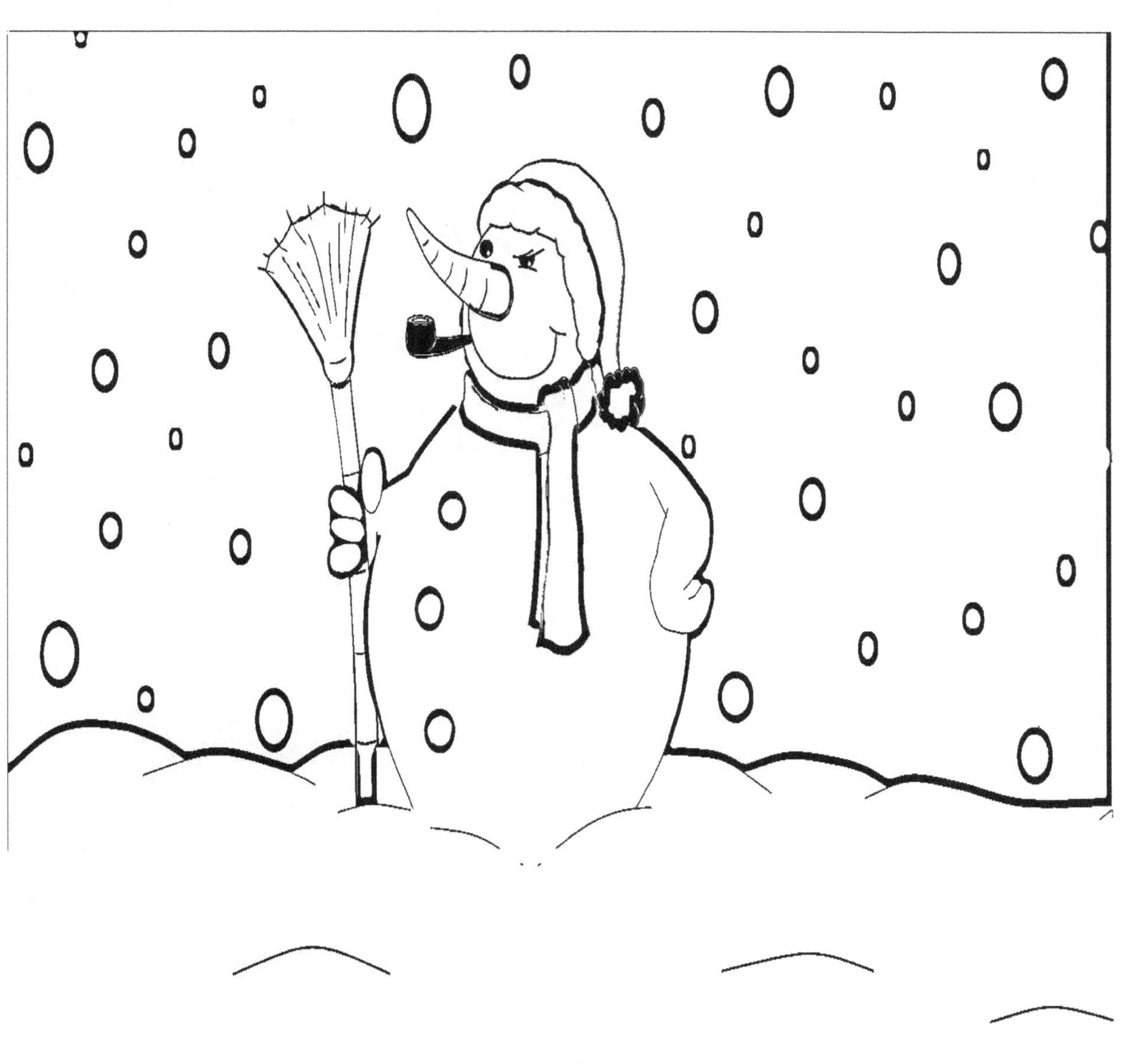

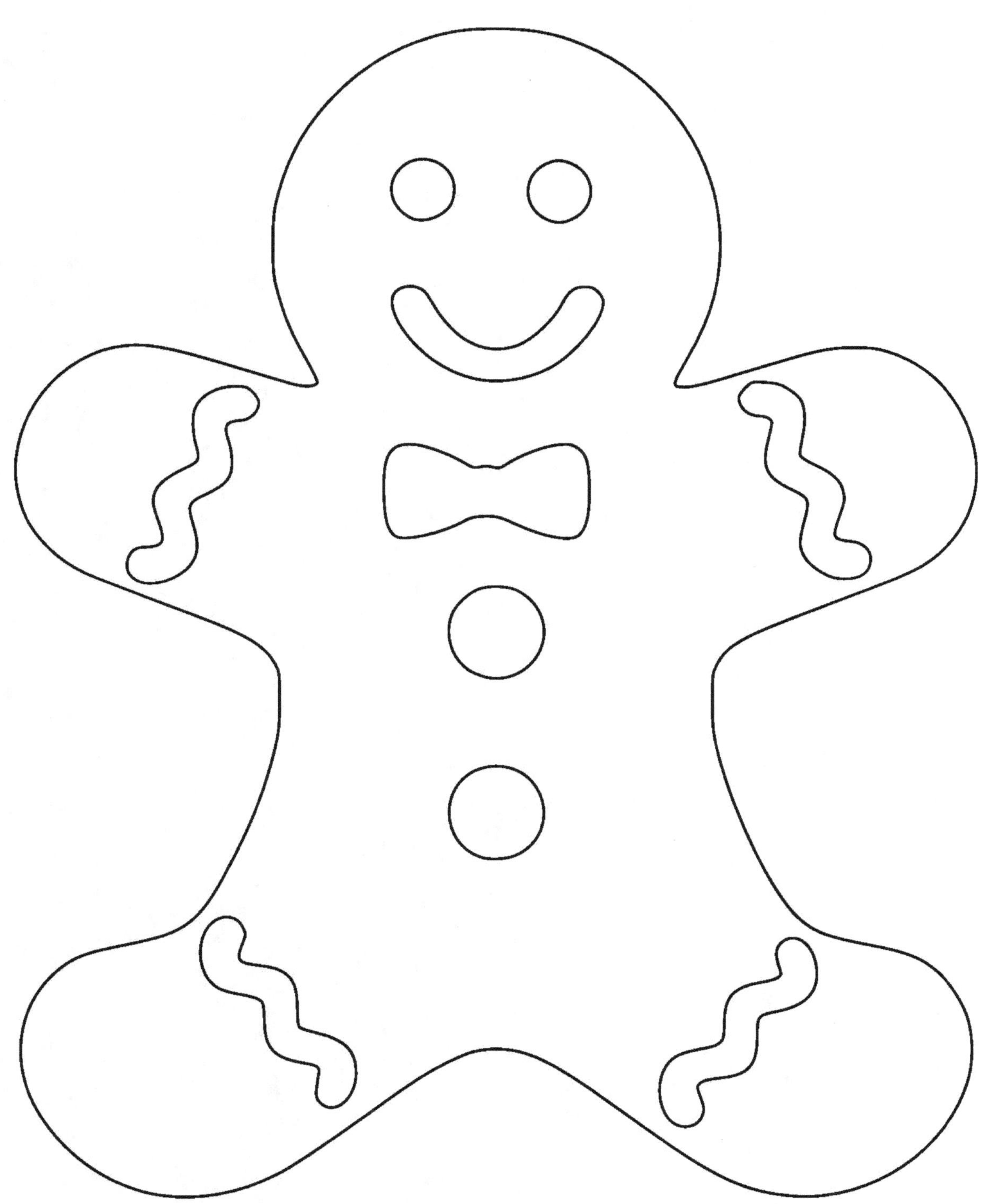

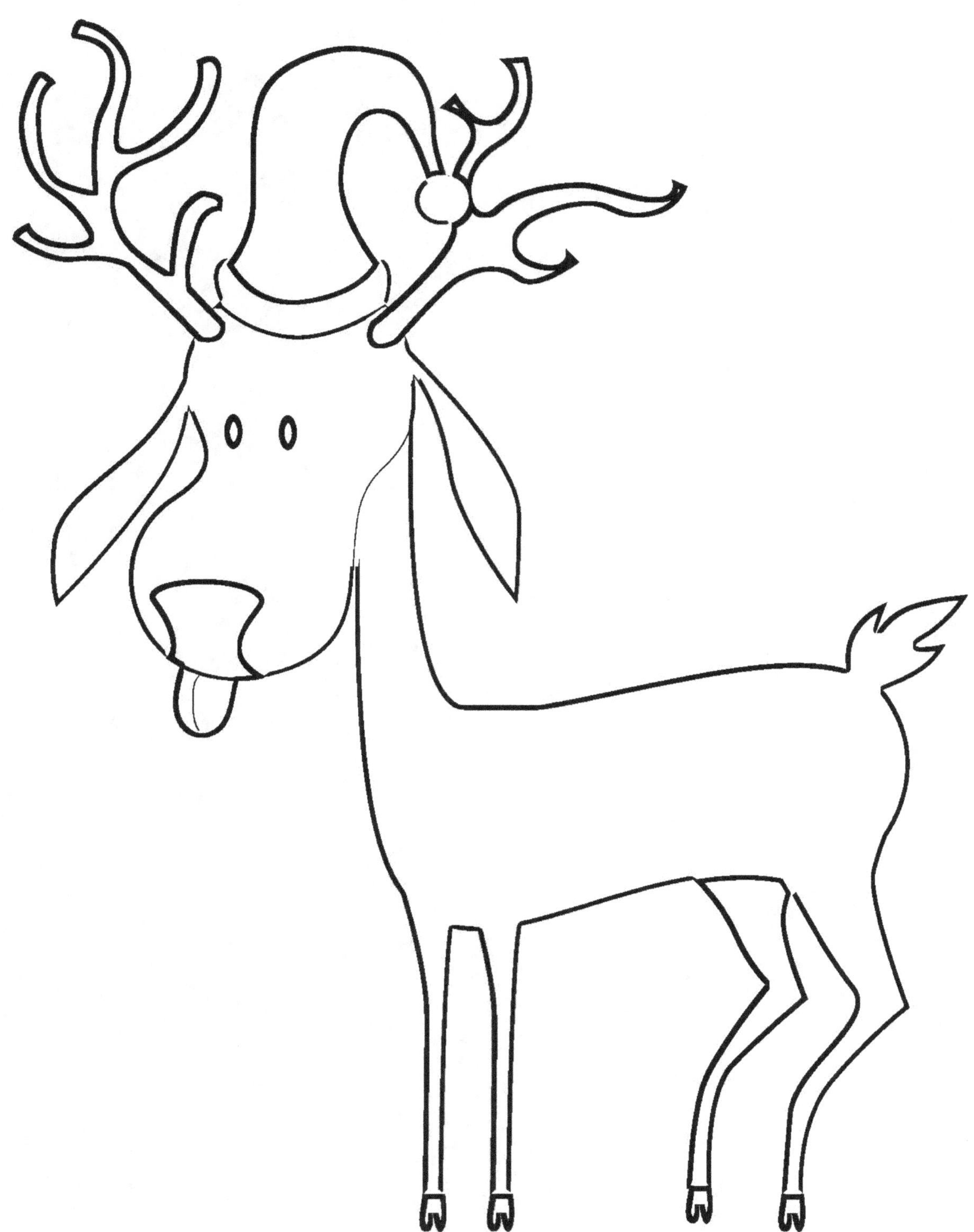

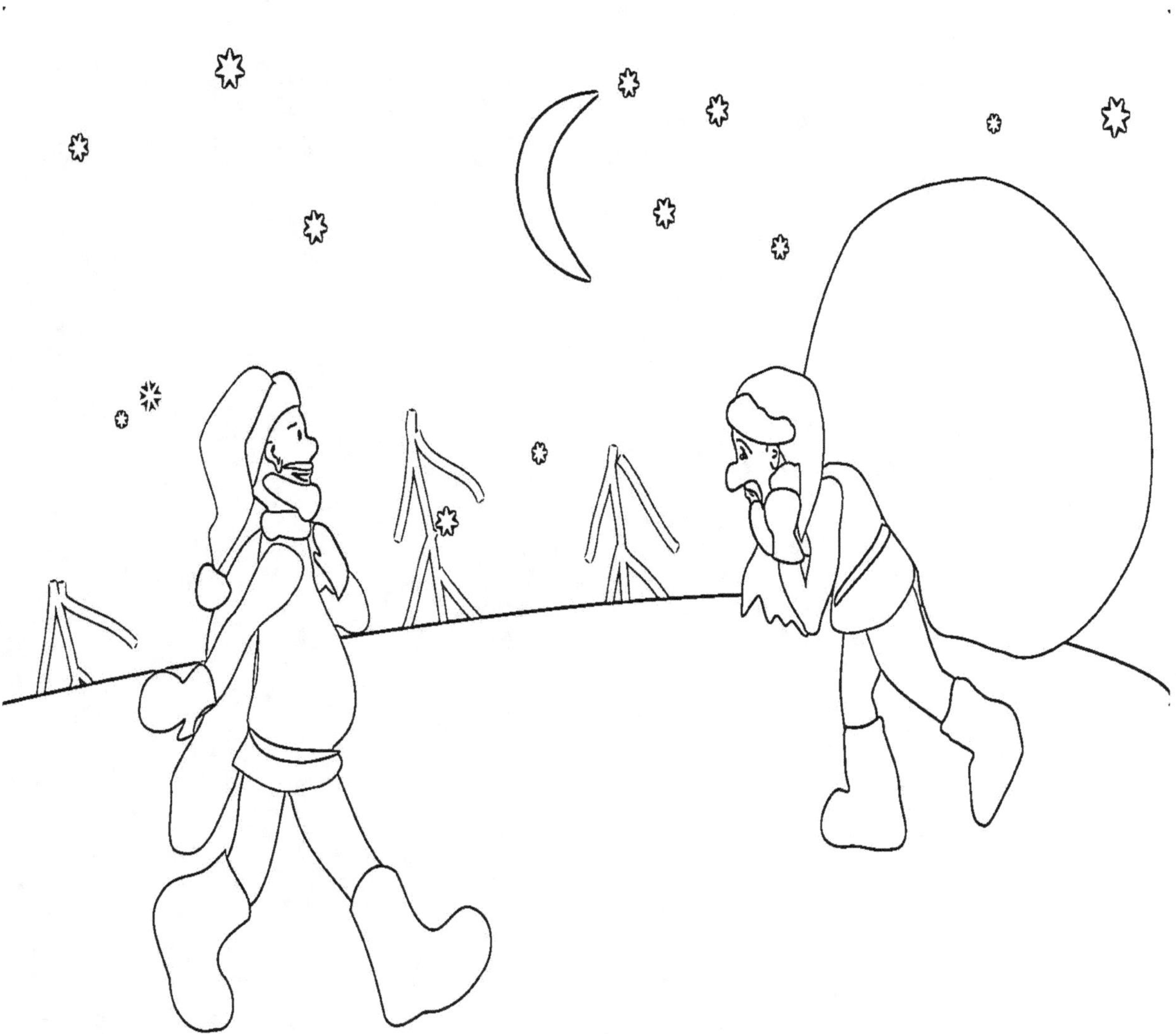

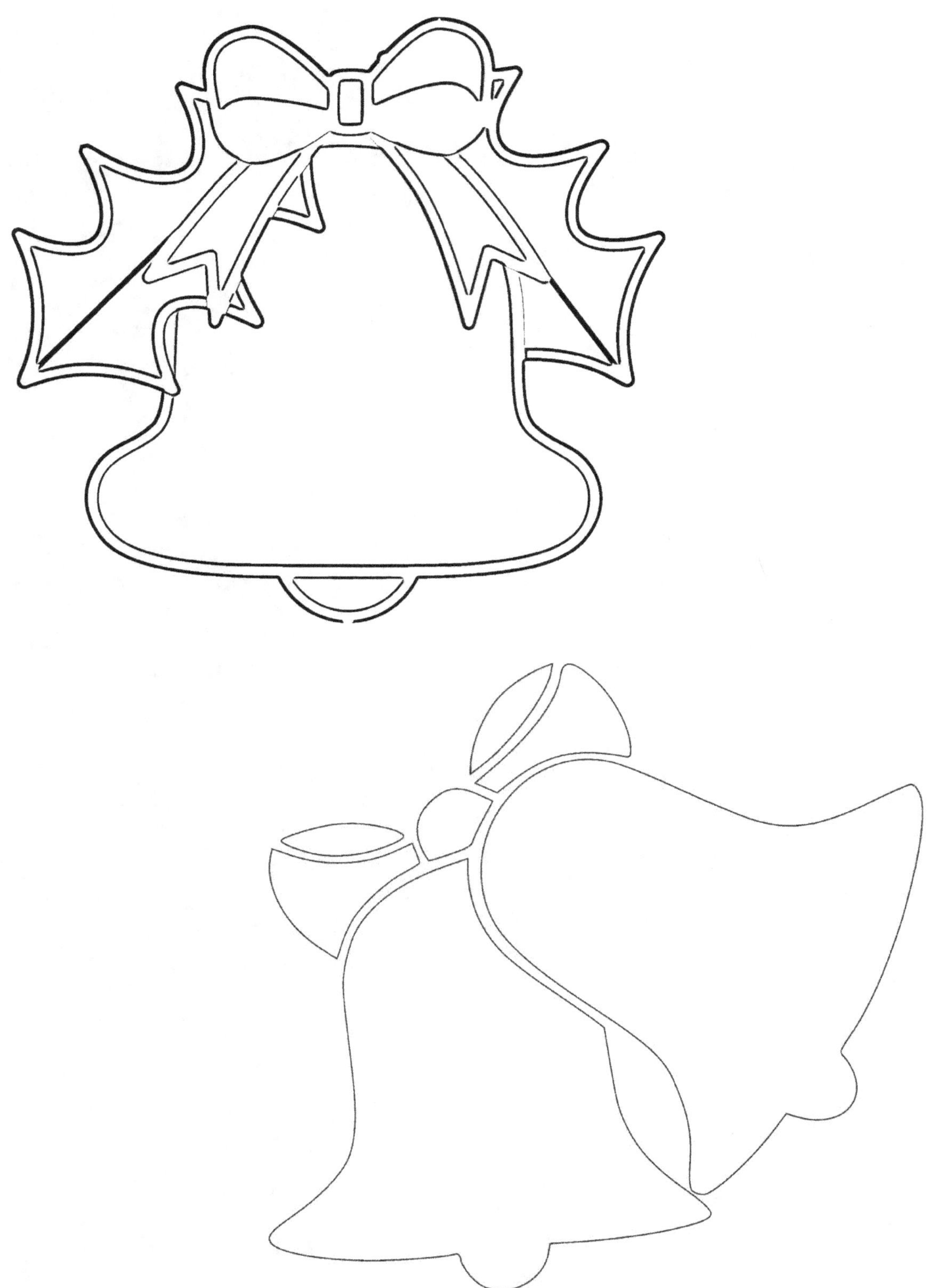

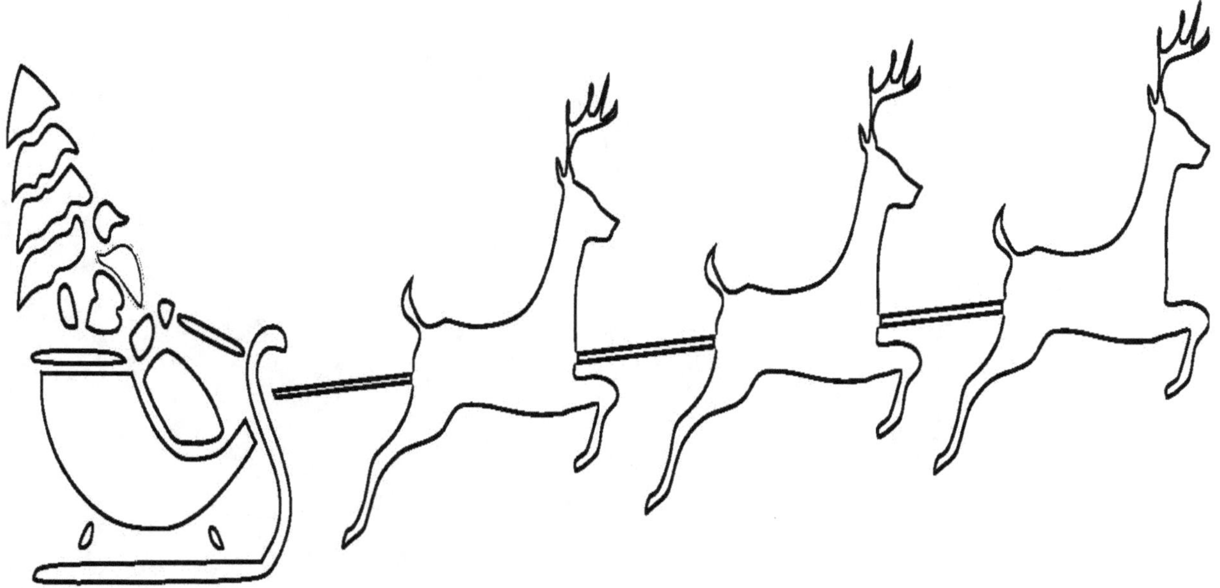

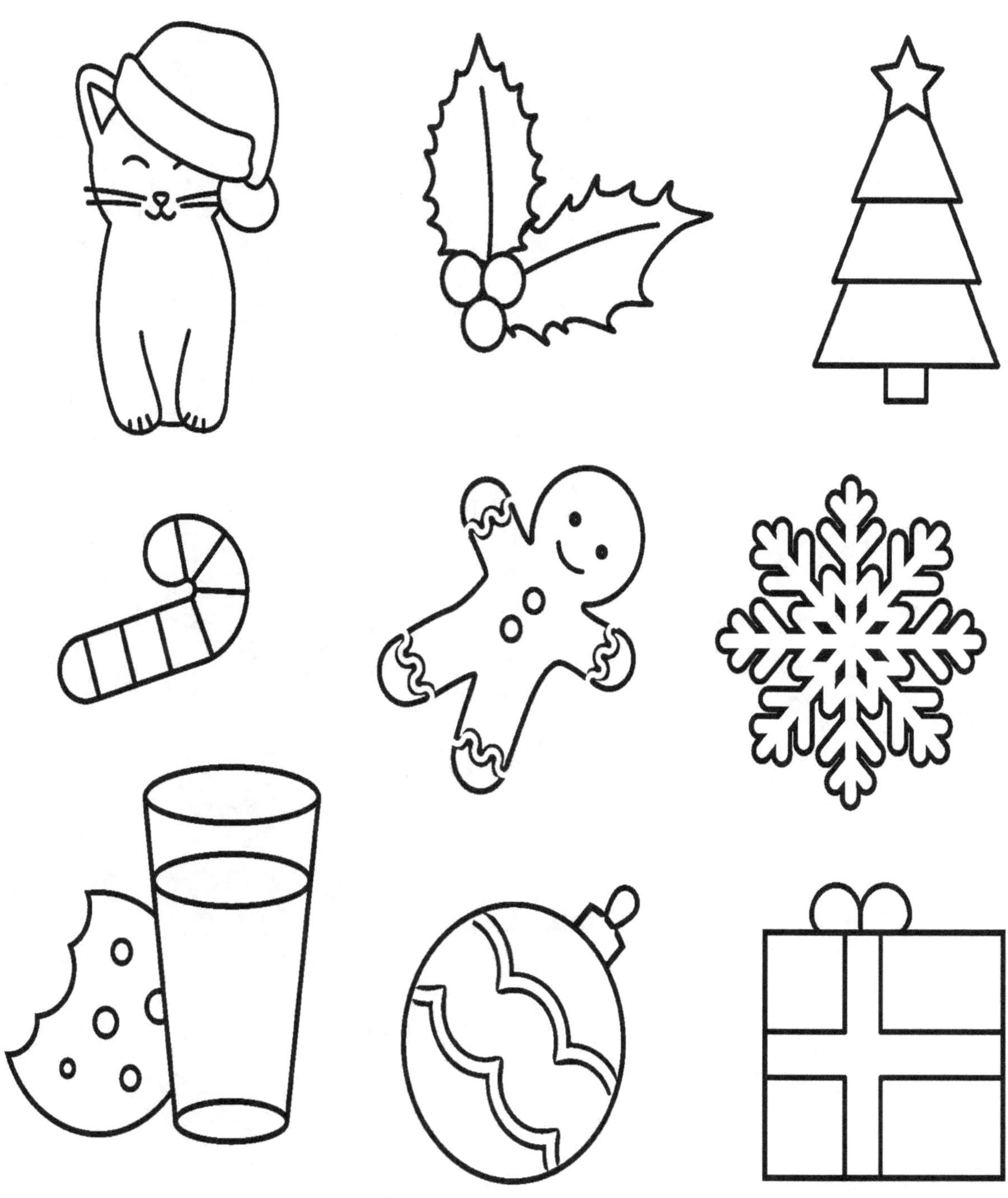

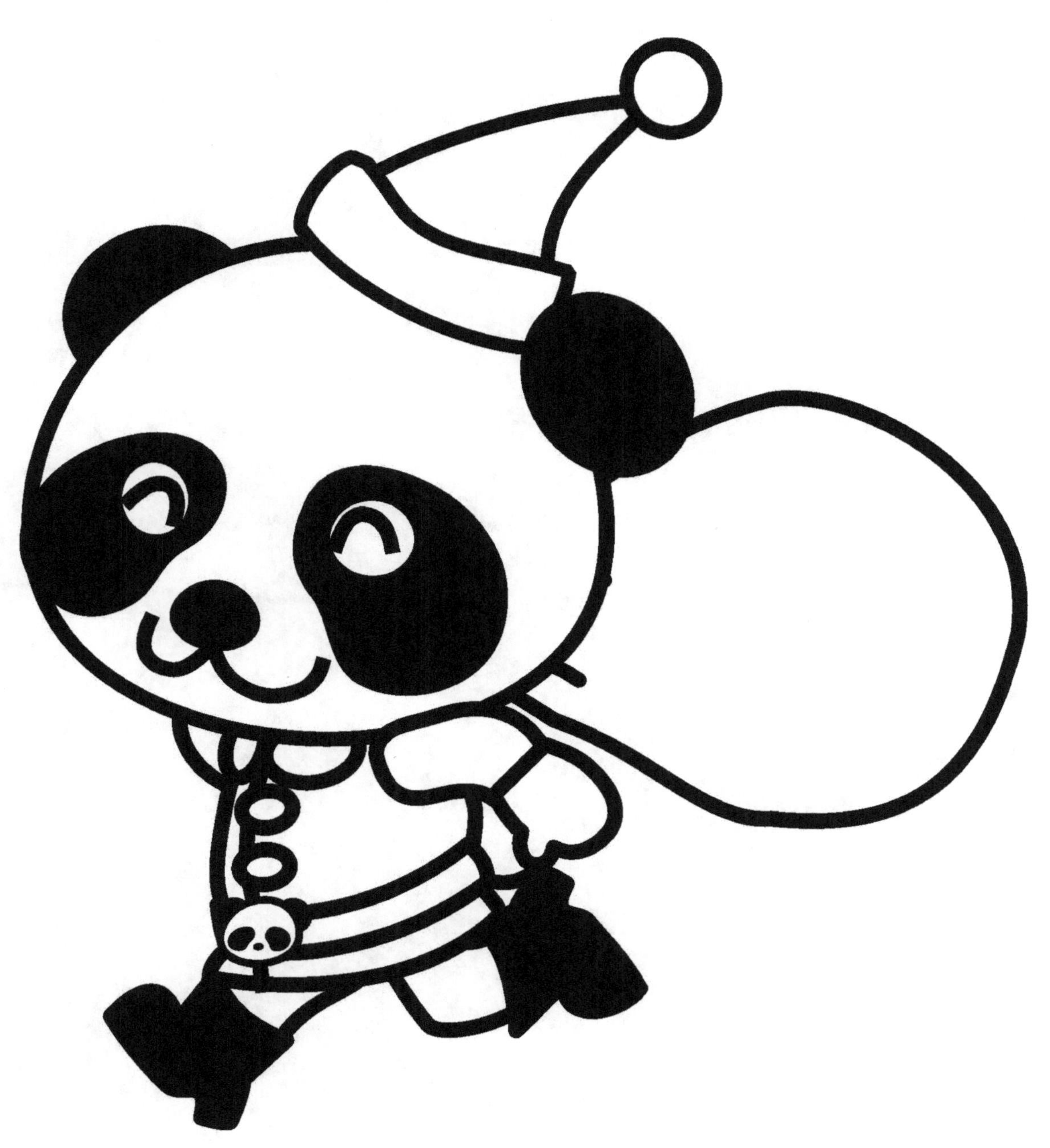

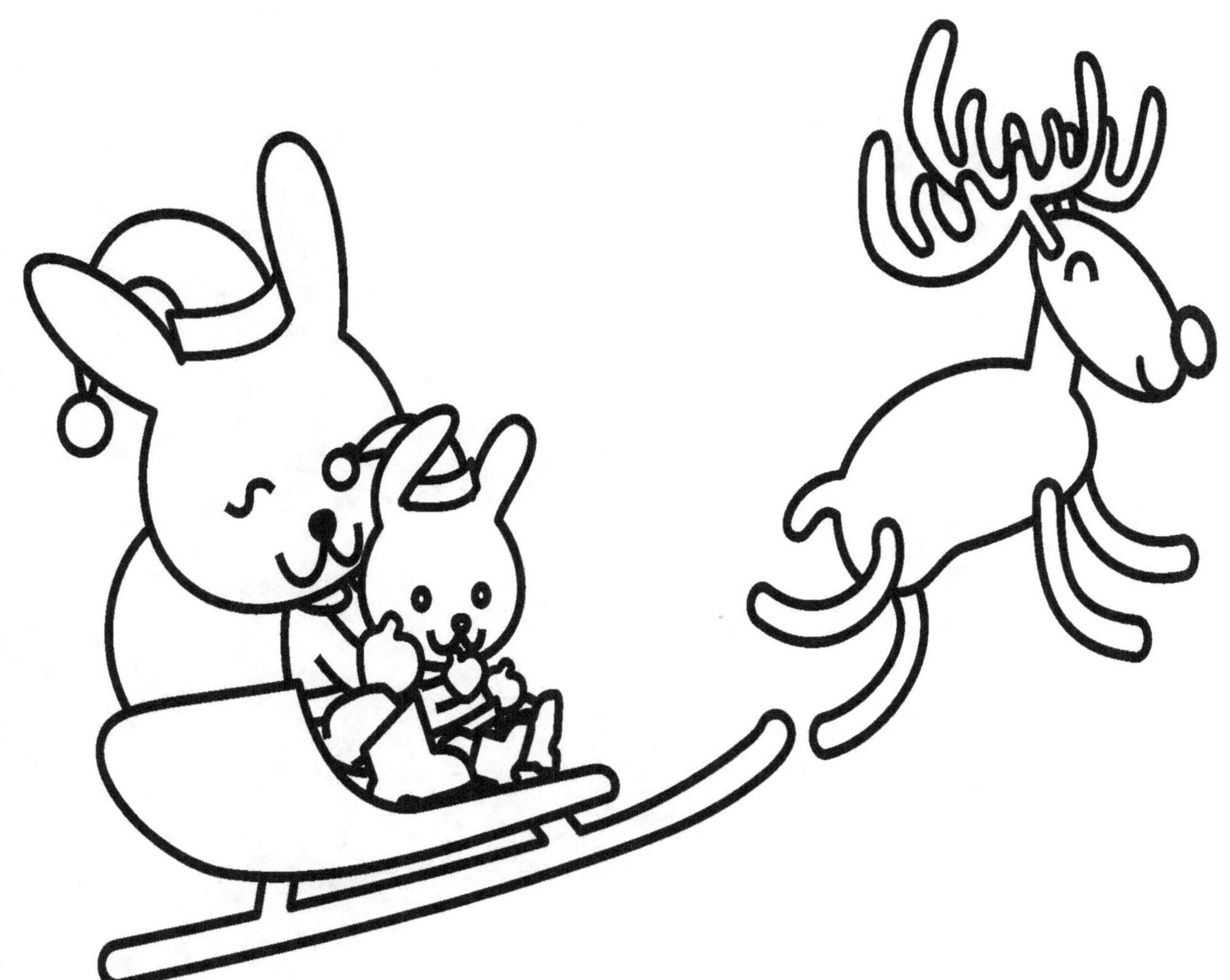

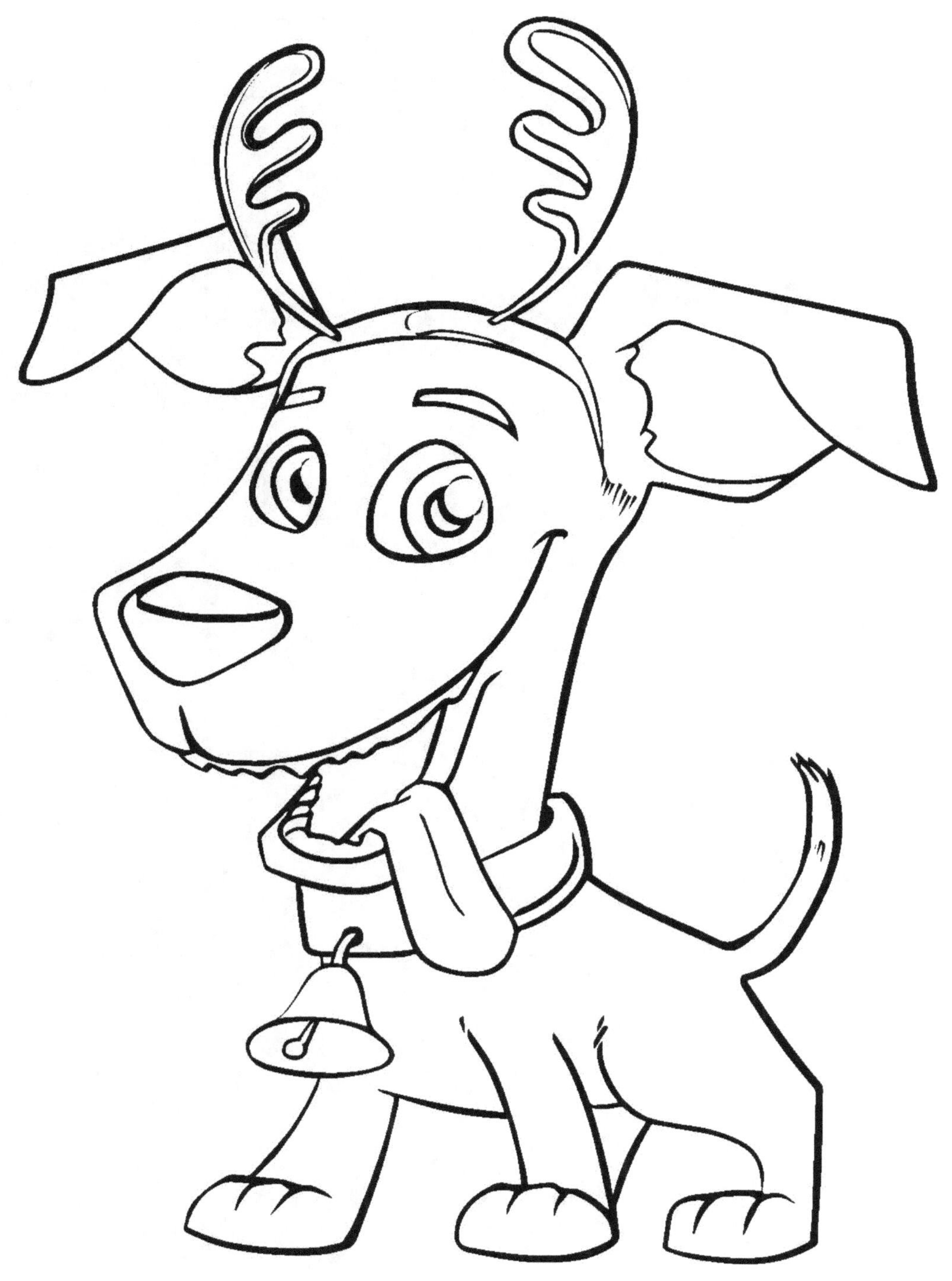

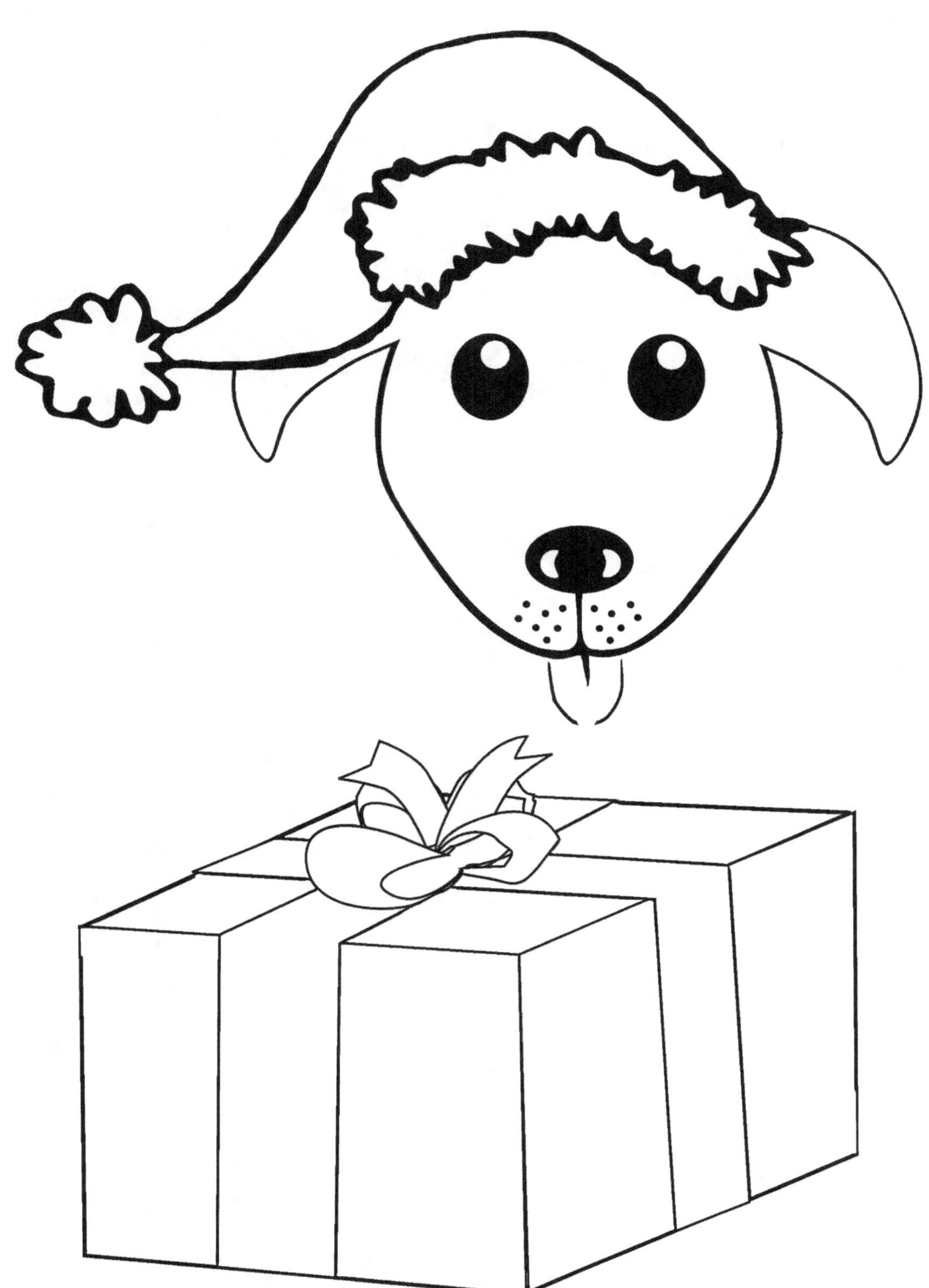

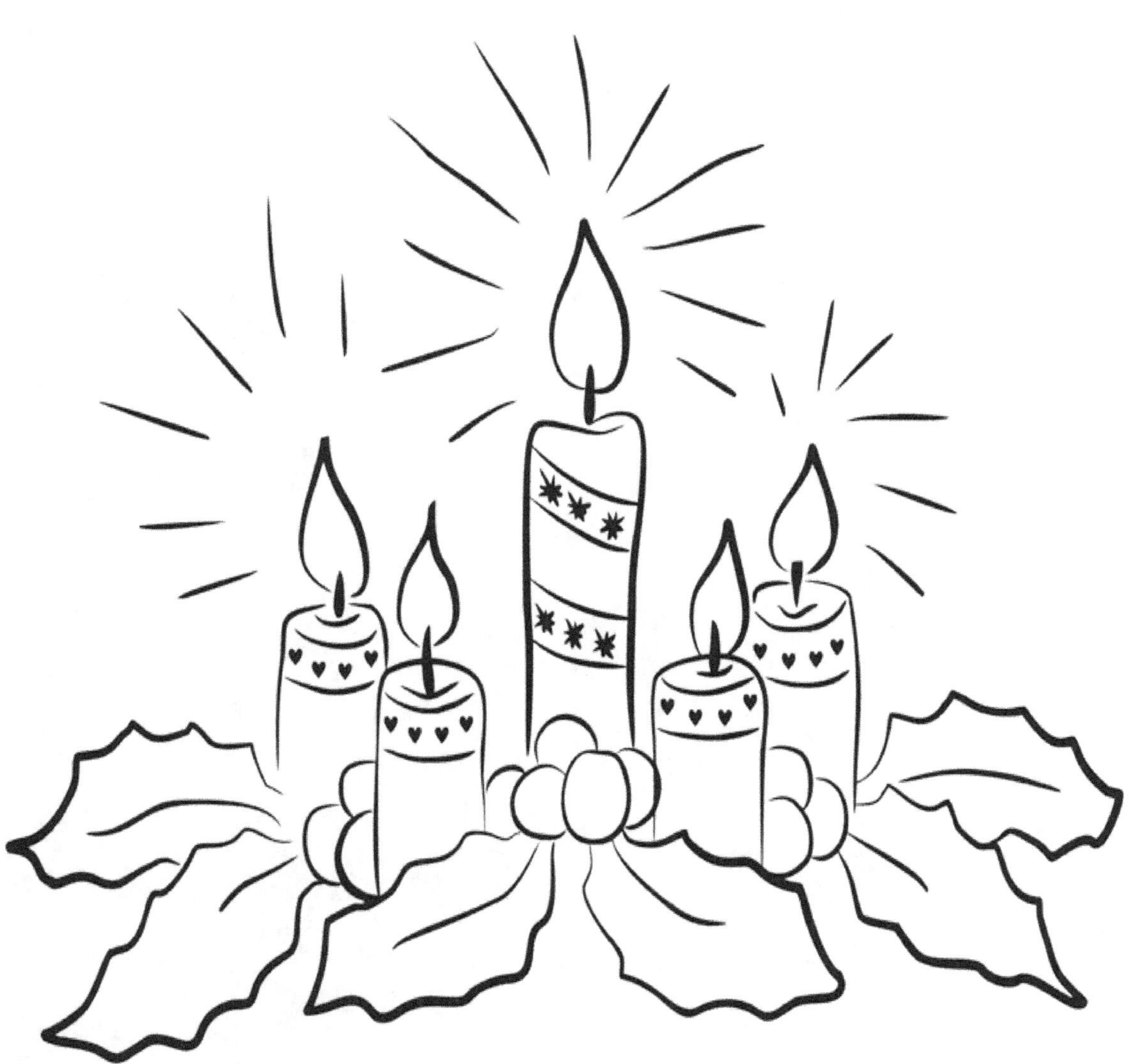

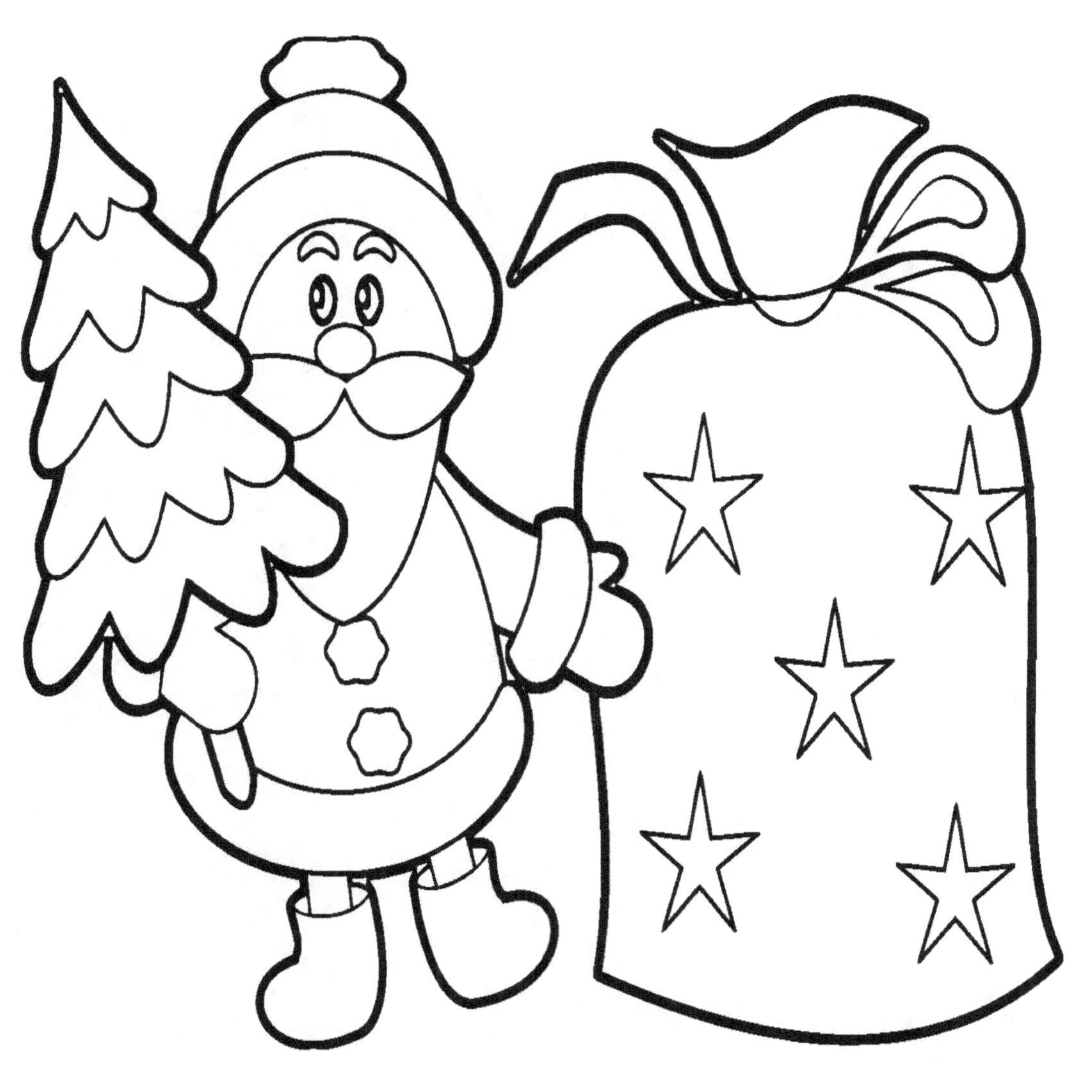

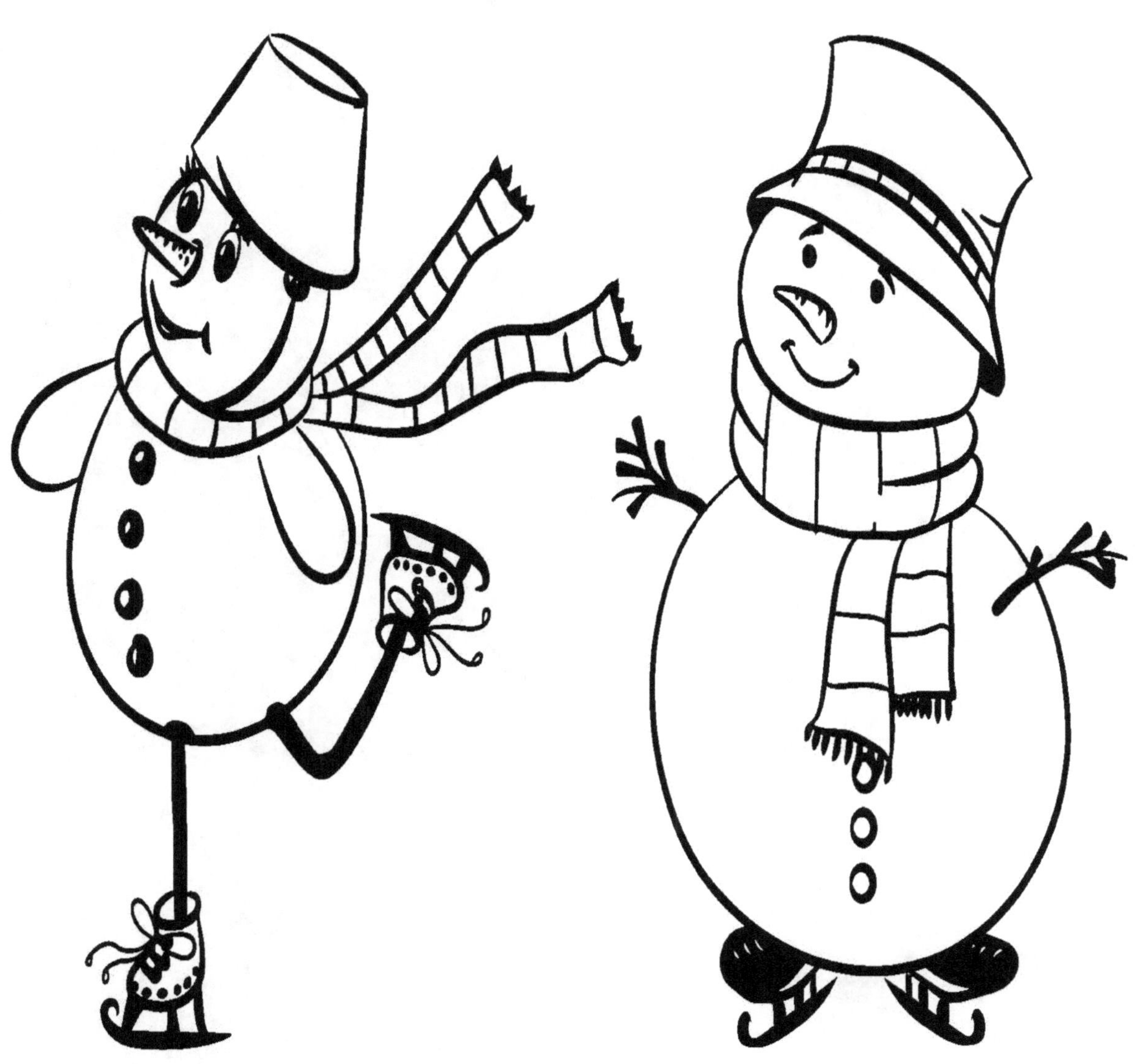

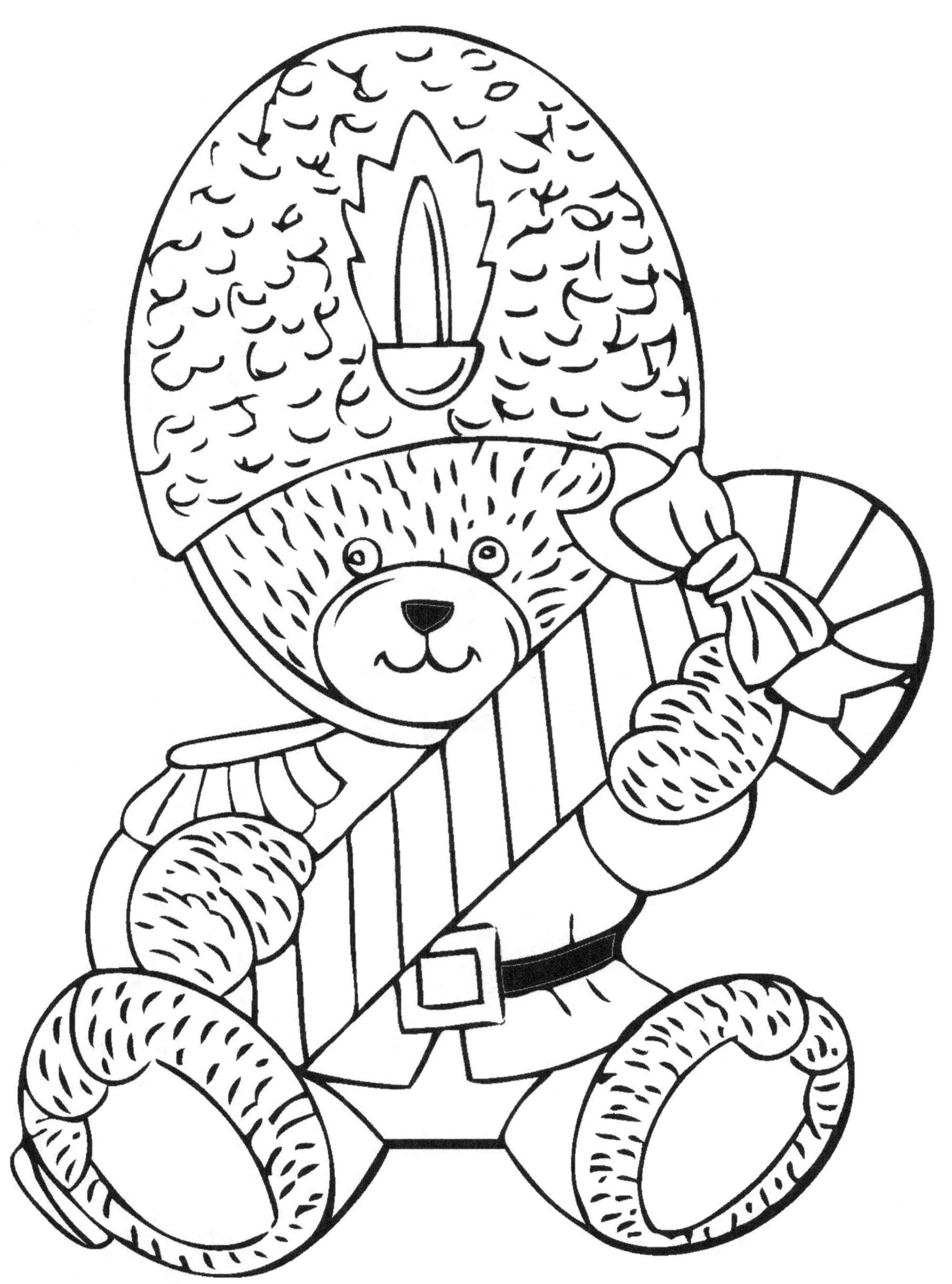

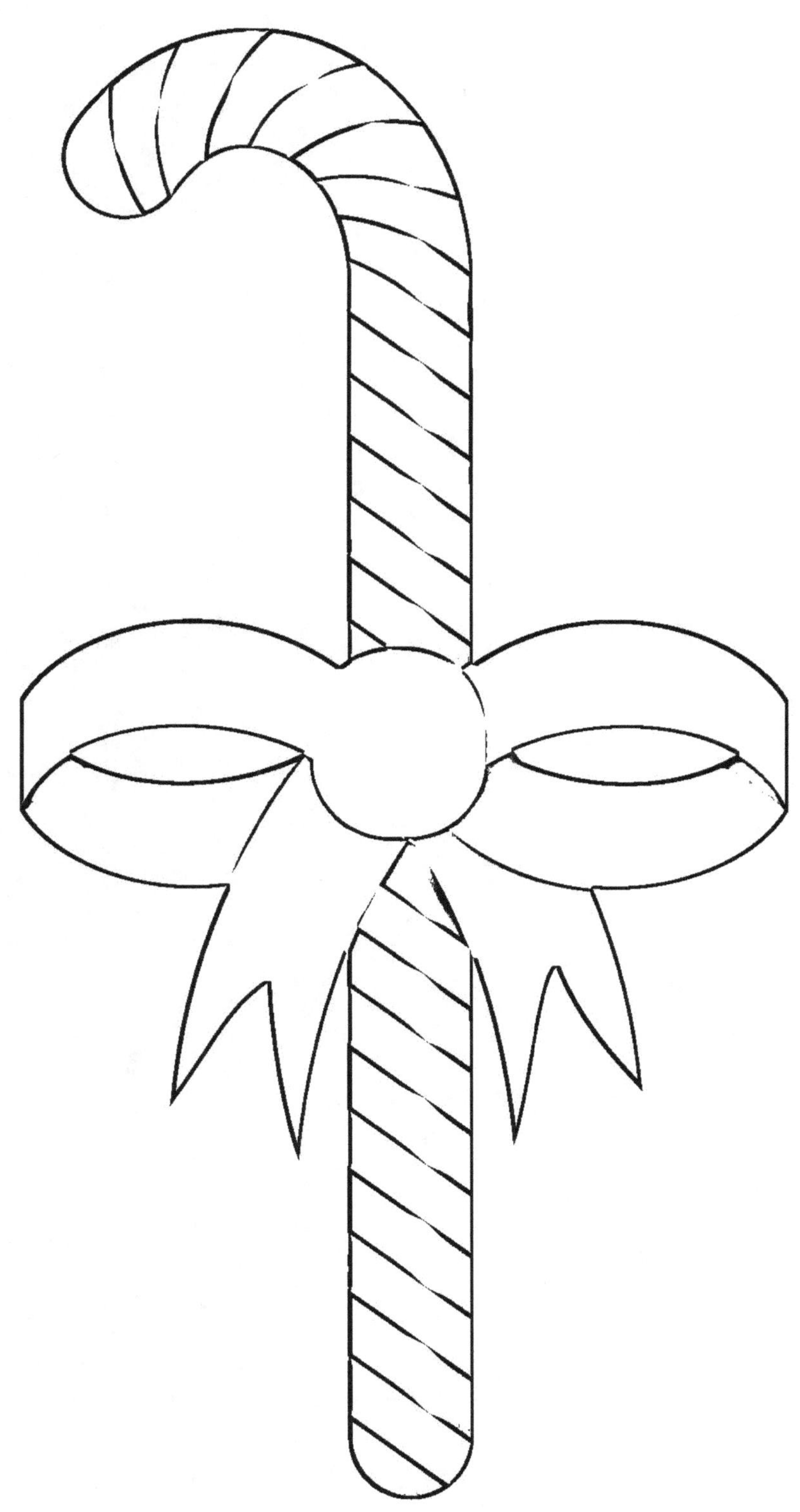

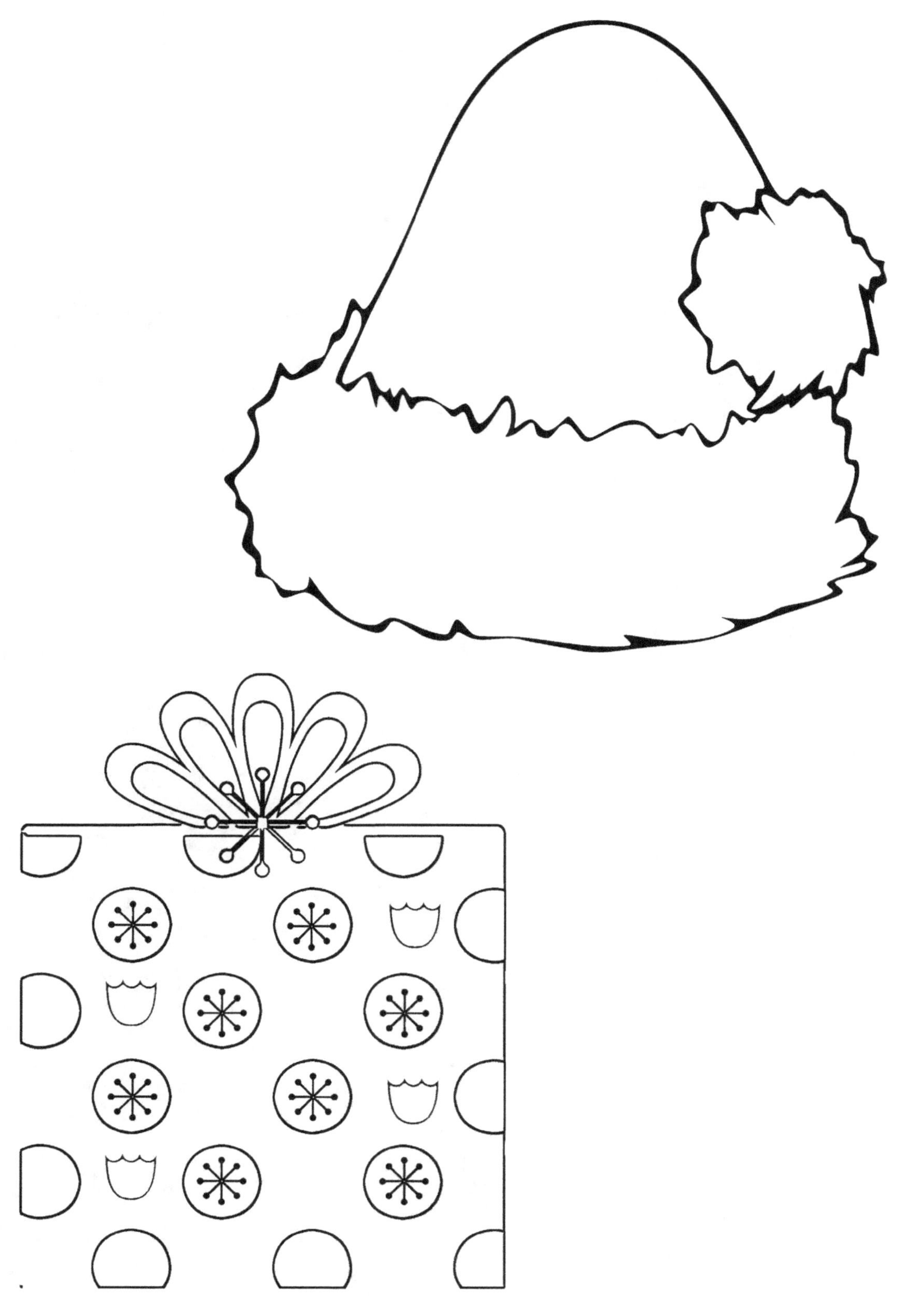